Happy
The Christmas Squirrel

by Juergen Wieshoff

For Victoria & Petra

In a forest, green and wide,
Lived young Happy, full of pride.
A squirrel keen, with fluffy tail,
Through woods and fields, he‘d eagerly sail.

Nuts were his treasure, his heart‘s delight,
He‘d gather them from morning till night.
But something new was soon to appear,
A Christmas change, filled with cheer.

Snowflakes danced, the air grew cold,
As Christmas tales of old were told.
Happy watched with curious eyes,
Underneath the winter skies.

He heard of treats, sweet and rare,
Beyond the nuts found everywhere.
"I must find these," he thought with glee,
"What wonders these rare sweets must be!"

Through the snow, Happy sped,
Dreams of sweets danced in his head.
He searched high and low, with hope in his heart,
For the Christmas treats, an essential part.

Of a world unknown, so rich and sweet,
Different from his usual treat.
But where to find these delights?
He pondered on cold winter nights.

Then one eve, by moon's soft light,
He saw a village, glowing bright.
Windows twinkled with festive glow,
A sight to see in the sparkling snow.

He crept closer, quiet as air,
Wondering what he'd find there.
In each window, a magical scene,
Of Christmas joy, calm and serene.

In one house, by a crackling fire,
Happy saw something to admire.
A tree adorned with lights and stars,
Underneath, sweets in jars.

His tiny heart beat fast and loud,
As he gazed upon the crowd.
Of gingerbread and candy canes,
And chocolate trains, leaving sugary lanes.

Happy's nose twitched, his eyes grew wide,
At the sweets he saw inside.
He made a plan, brave and bold,
To taste these treats, of old tales told.

He scampered up the snowy wall,
Careful not to slip or fall.
Through a window, slightly ajar,
Happy entered, like a star.

Inside the house, all was still,
He moved forward, with a thrill.
The Christmas tree, grand and tall,
Underneath, sweets enthral.

Gingerbread men with icing lace,
Chocolate coins, a sugary space.
Happy‘s heart danced with joy,
Like a child with a new toy.

**He tasted a cookie, then two, then three,
Each bite filled with ecstasy.
Never had he known such flavor,
Every morsel, he wished to savor.**

**But then he heard a sound, a stir,
And hid behind the Christmas fir.
A family entered, with smiles so wide,
Happy watched them, from where he did hide.**

Their laughter filled the room with cheer,
Spreading the warmth of Christmas near.
Happy felt a glow inside,
From the joy he could not hide.

He realized then, in that warm place,
Christmas was more than a sweet embrace.
It was love, and joy, and family tight,
That made the Christmas spirit bright.

Quietly, Happy slipped away,
Back to the forest, before day‘s first ray.
With a heart full of new-found love,
And the stars twinkling above.

He gathered nuts, his old delight,
But remembered the sweets from the night.
A mix of old and new he‘d bring,
To the forest, for a Christmas fling.

Back in the woods, with his friends so dear,
Happy shared his tales of cheer.
Of the village, the sweets, the joy he found,
In the warmth of Christmas abound.

His friends listened, eyes aglow,
Amazed at the tale of snow.
They felt the Christmas spirit rise,
Under the starry winter skies.

Together, they prepared a feast,
For every bird and every beast.
Nuts and berries, sweets so fine,
Under the giant Christmas pine.

The forest was alive with glee,
As they decorated their own tree.
With berries red and nuts so brown,
Their Christmas joy knew no bound.

The night of Christmas Eve arrived,
The forest seemed magically contrived.
Snowflakes fell, soft and light,
Blanketing the woods in white.

Animals gathered, round the tree,
United in festive glee.
Happy‘s eyes shone bright and clear,
For the Christmas moment was finally here.

They sang songs of old and new,
Under the sky so deep and blue.
Happy felt his heart swell with pride,
For the joy he could not hide.

He shared his sweets, so rare and fine,
Under the moon‘s soft, silver shine.
His friends marveled at the taste,
No single crumb went to waste.

The owls hooted in rhythmic tunes,
Under the glow of the winter moon.
Rabbits danced with merry leaps,
While the foxes played in joyful heaps.

Happy watched with a happy sigh,
Underneath the starlit sky.
This Christmas was special, he could tell,
In his heart, joy did swell.

Then from above, a sound so clear,
Rang through the night, drawing near.
A jingle of bells, a soft hoof prance,
Caught every animal's glance.

Down from the sky, with a sleigh so bright,
Came Santa Claus, in the night.
His eyes twinkled with a merry gleam,
Like the whisper of a dream.

„Hello, Happy," Santa said,
With a gentle nod of his head.
„I've heard of your quest for sweets so grand,
And your journey through the snowy land."

Happy blushed, a little shy,
Underneath the Christmas sky.
Santa laughed, a sound so merry,
Like the chirp of a berry.

He gave Happy a small, wrapped gift,
That gave his spirits an extra lift.
Inside was a mix of nuts and sweets,
A perfect blend of Christmas treats.

„Remember, Happy," Santa said with a smile,
„Christmas joy lasts more than just a while.
It's about love, and giving, and friends so dear,
And carrying this spirit throughout the year."

Santa waved and off he flew,
Into the night, out of view.
The animals cheered, their hearts light,
On that magical Christmas night.

Happy felt a tear of joy,
For the lessons learned, not just a toy.
He understood now, clear and true,
What Christmas really meant to do.

The party continued, full of cheer,
With Happy and his friends so dear.
They shared stories, laughed, and played,
In the beautiful forest glade.

As dawn approached, with light so mild,
Each animal felt like a child.
With hearts full of Christmas spirit,
A night they‘d always cherish, every bit.

As the sun rose on Christmas day,
The forest woke in a joyful way.
Happy, with his fluffy tail,
Knew this Christmas tale would never stale.

He had found joy in something new,
But remembered the old, like morning dew.
In his heart, he found a balance,
Of tradition and new experiences.

Now every year, when snowflakes fall,
Happy remembers the Christmas call.
Of sweets and nuts, friends and cheer,
In the most wonderful time of year.

In the forest, green and wide,
Lives Happy, with pride inside.
A squirrel who found Christmas joy,
More precious than any toy.

The End

About the book:
Join Happy, the curious and spirited squirrel, on a magical Christmas journey in „Happy the Christmas Squirrel." In this heartwarming tale, set in a beautifully illustrated forest brimming with wonder, our fluffy-tailed hero discovers the joys of Christmas in a way he never expected.

Happy has always loved nuts, gathering them with joy in the lush green forest he calls home. But this Christmas, as snowflakes dust the woodland and festive lights twinkle in the distant village, Happy's curiosity leads him to a world of new delights. From the cozy warmth of a village home to the sweet surprises under a twinkling Christmas tree, Happy's adventure is filled with new tastes, new sights, and new friends.

But what will he learn from this journey? Can the joy of Christmas sweets match the love he has for his traditional nutty delights? Happy's adventure will teach him the importance of balancing the old with the new, and the true meaning of Christmas spirit.

An enchanting tale with both classic and contemporary illustrations, perfect for young readers and families to enjoy together over the festive season. It's a story of discovery, friendship and the timeless magic of Christmas.

About the Author:
Juergen Wieshoff is not only a talented author but also a devoted father and loving husband. Inspired by the vivid imagination of his daughter Victoria and the unwavering support of his wife Petra, Juergen embarked on a journey to create a world of wonder and joy through his writing.

With a background rich in storytelling and a heart full of family love, Juergen crafted „Happy the Christmas Squirrel" as a testament to the joys of family life and the magic of the holiday season. This book is a special tribute to his beloved wife Petra, embodying the warmth, laughter, and love that fills their home.

Juergen's unique voice as an author combines the innocence and curiosity of childhood with the wisdom and depth of adulthood, making his stories a delightful read for all ages. His ability to see the world through the eyes of both a father and a child brings a special charm and relatability to his work.

When he's not weaving tales of fantasy and adventure, Juergen enjoys spending quality time with his family, exploring the great outdoors, and capturing life's little moments with his daughter Victoria, who continues to be his greatest source of inspiration and joy.

„Happy the Christmas Squirrel" is more than just a book; it's a piece of Juergen's heart, shared with the world. With each page, he hopes to spread the warmth and joy of his family's love to every reader.